YOU CAN DRAW IT!
DOGS

WRITTEN BY JON EPPARD
ILLUSTRATED BY STEVE PORTER

BELLWETHER MEDIA • MINNEAPOLIS, MN

This edition first published in 2013 by Bellwether Media, Inc.

No part of this publication may be reproduced in whole or in part without written permission of the publisher. For information regarding permission, write to Bellwether Media, Inc., Attention: Permissions Department, 5357 Penn Avenue South, Minneapolis, MN 55419.

Library of Congress Cataloging-in-Publication Data

Eppard, Jon.
 Dogs / by Jon Eppard.
      pages cm – (You can draw it!)
 Includes bibliographical references and index.
 Summary: "Information accompanies step-by-step instructions on how to draw dogs. The text level and subject matter is intended for students in grades 3 through 7"–Provided by publisher.
  ISBN 978-1-60014-810-1 (hardcover : alk. paper)
  ISBN 978-1-60014-855-2 (paperback : alk. paper)
 1. Dogs in art–Juvenile literature. 2. Drawing–Technique–Juvenile literature. I. Title.
  NC783.8.D64E67 2012
  743.6'9772–dc23
                    2012017227

Text copyright © 2013 by Bellwether Media, Inc. PILOT, EXPRESS, and associated logos are trademarks and/or registered trademarks of Bellwether Media, Inc. SCHOLASTIC, CHILDREN'S PRESS, and associated logos are trademarks and/or registered trademarks of Scholastic Inc.

Printed in the United States of America, North Mankato, MN.

TABLE OF CONTENTS

Dogs! 4
Pug 6
Saint Bernard 8
Beagle 10
Labrador Retriever 12
Dalmatian 14
Doberman Pinscher 16
German Shepherd 18
Chihuahua 20
Glossary 22
To Learn More 23
Index 24

DOGS!

Many people believe that dogs were the first animals to be **domesticated** by humans. For thousands of years, dogs have been helping humans hunt, **herd**, protect, and serve. They have earned their reputation as "man's best friend."

DRAWING FROM PHOTOS IS A GREAT PLACE TO START. WORK YOUR WAY UP TO DRAWING FROM MEMORY OR YOUR IMAGINATION.

Before you begin drawing, you will need a few basic supplies.

PAPER

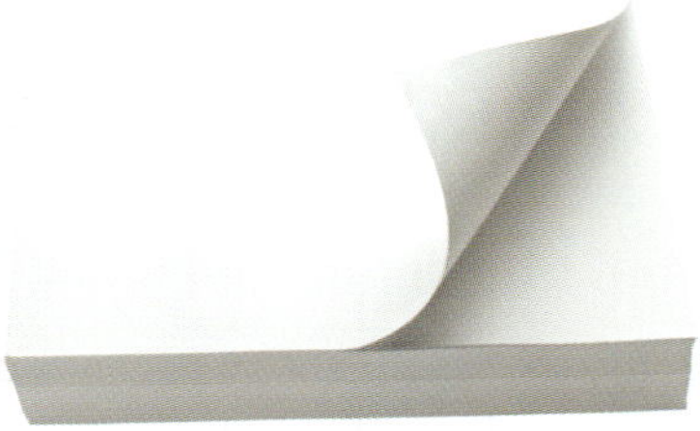

DRAWING PENCILS

BLACK INK PEN

2B OR NOT 2B?

NOT ALL DRAWING PENCILS ARE THE SAME. "B" PENCILS ARE SOFTER, MAKE DARKER MARKS, AND SMUDGE EASILY. "H" PENCILS ARE HARDER, MAKE LIGHTER MARKS, AND DON'T SMUDGE VERY MUCH AT ALL.

COLORED PENCILS
(ALL DRAWINGS IN THIS BOOK WERE FINISHED WITH COLORED PENCILS.)

ERASER

PENCIL SHARPENER

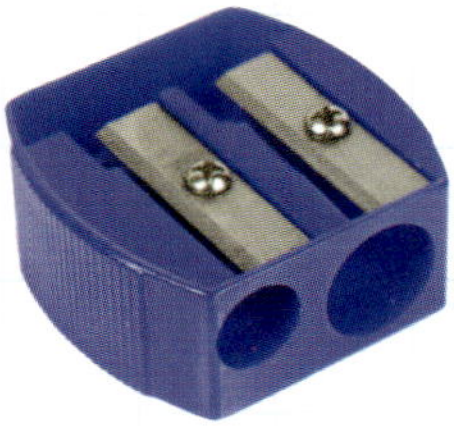

Pug
The Distinguished Dog

Pugs are one of the oldest dog breeds in the world. They originated in ancient China and later became popular pets for royal families in Europe. Today Pugs are loved for their deep wrinkles and playful personalities. Their flattened **muzzles** make breathing difficult, but that doesn't stop Pugs from showing off their energy and **agility**.

1 BEGIN BY STACKING TWO CIRCLES AND AN OVAL

2 LIGHTLY ADD TRIANGLES FOR THE EARS AND LINES FOR THE LEGS AND PAWS

BREAK IT DOWN

JUST ABOUT ANY SUBJECT YOU'RE DRAWING CAN BE BROKEN DOWN INTO SMALLER PARTS. LOOK FOR CIRCLES, OVALS, SQUARES, AND OTHER BASIC SHAPES THAT CAN HELP BUILD YOUR DRAWING.

DRAW THE EYES, NOSE, AND MOUTH

ADD DETAIL TO THE MUZZLE AND PAWS

ADD THE OUTLINE OF THE LEGS AND PAWS

DRAW THE FOLDS OF SKIN ON THE FACE AND BODY

 AND COLOR

PUGS ARE USUALLY TAN OR BLACK. MOST PUGS HAVE BLACK AROUND THEIR MUZZLE AND EARS.

Saint Bernard
The Rescue Dog

With both size and smarts, Saint Bernards are a capable breed. They were first used as guard dogs and to rescue people lost in the cold mountains of Europe. Today they excel in the dog sport of **weight pulling**. Their protective nature and loyalty also make them great family pets!

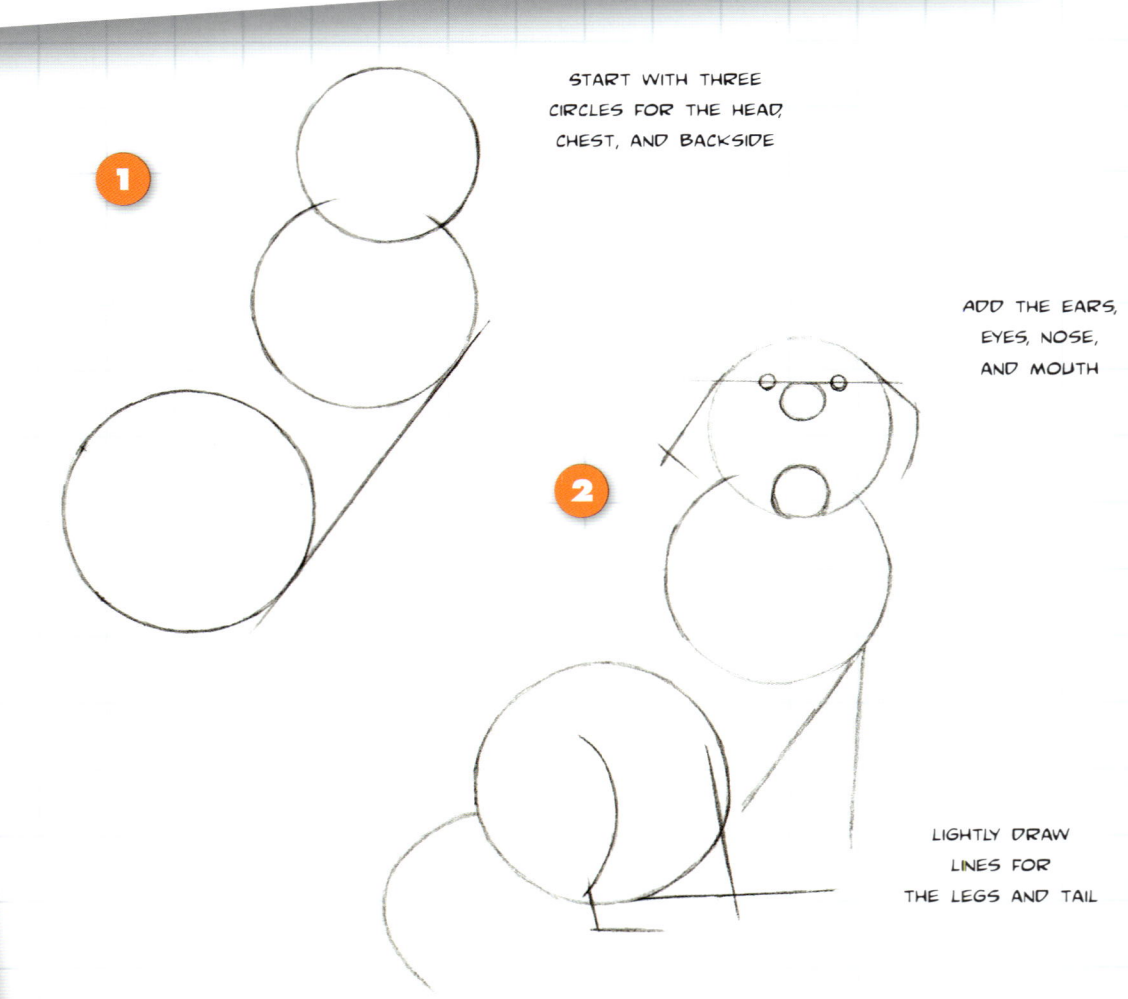

1. START WITH THREE CIRCLES FOR THE HEAD, CHEST, AND BACKSIDE
2. ADD THE EARS, EYES, NOSE, AND MOUTH

LIGHTLY DRAW LINES FOR THE LEGS AND TAIL

3 COMPLETE THE OUTLINE OF THE TAIL, LEGS, AND BODY

ADD DETAIL TO THE MOUTH

WHICH WAY TO GO?

IF YOU'RE LEFT-HANDED, START YOUR DRAWING FROM THE RIGHT. IF YOU'RE RIGHT-HANDED, START YOUR DRAWING FROM THE LEFT. THIS WILL HELP YOU AVOID SMUDGING.

4 ADD DETAILS TO THE FACE, EARS, AND PAWS

FINISH YOUR EDGES WITH JAGGED LINES TO CREATE LONG FUR

5 INK AND COLOR

SAINT BERNARDS ARE REDDISH BROWN AND WHITE. THEY USUALLY HAVE DARKER HAIR AROUND THE EYES, EARS, AND MUZZLE.

Beagle
The Scent Hound

Beagles, like all **scent hounds**, have a powerful sense of smell. These happy dogs with long, floppy ears love to find and follow scent trails. Some even work alongside humans. **Canine** members of the Beagle Brigade sniff luggage and packages at airports to keep banned food items out of the United States.

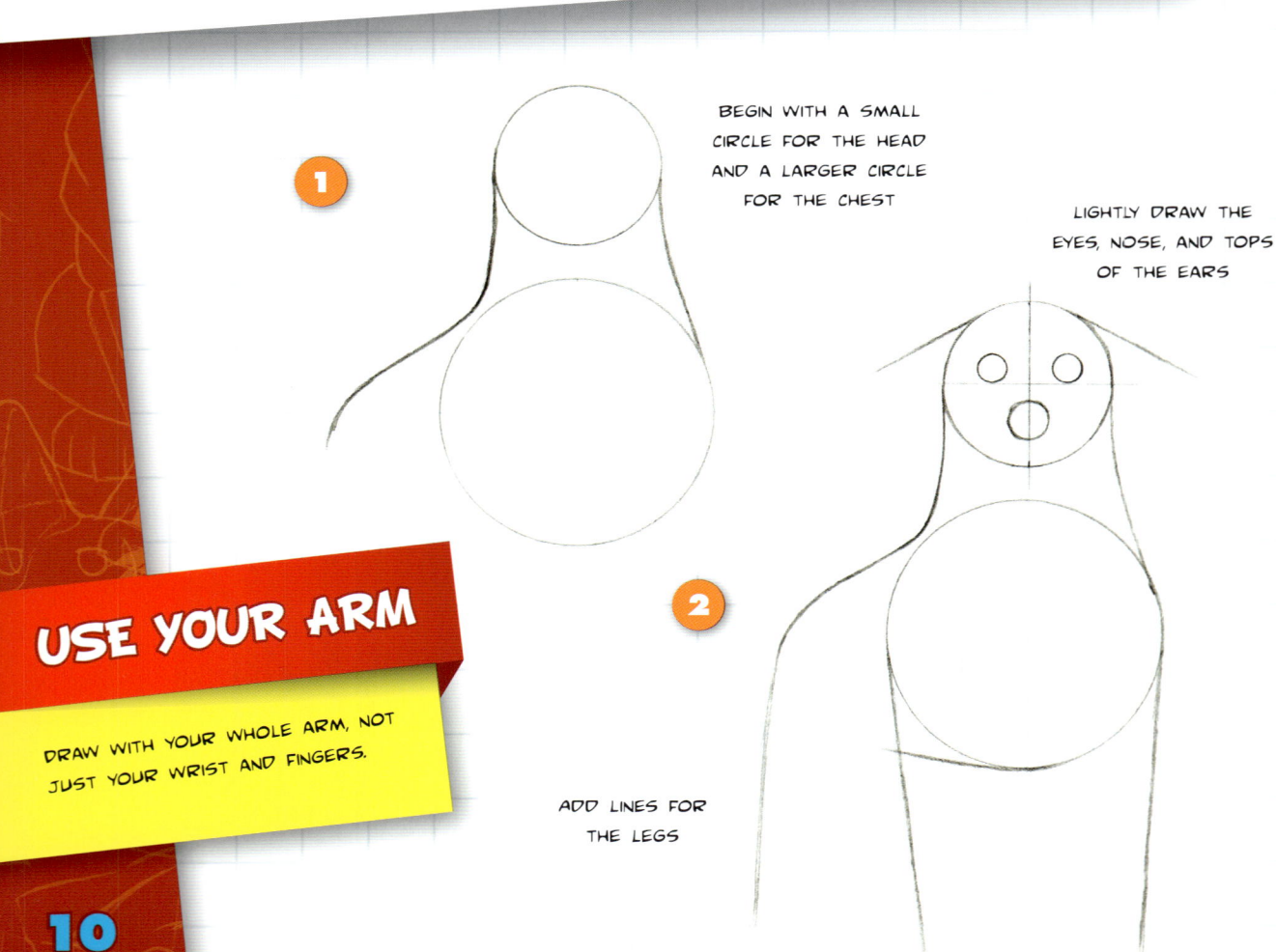

1 BEGIN WITH A SMALL CIRCLE FOR THE HEAD AND A LARGER CIRCLE FOR THE CHEST

2 LIGHTLY DRAW THE EYES, NOSE, AND TOPS OF THE EARS

ADD LINES FOR THE LEGS

USE YOUR ARM

DRAW WITH YOUR WHOLE ARM, NOT JUST YOUR WRIST AND FINGERS.

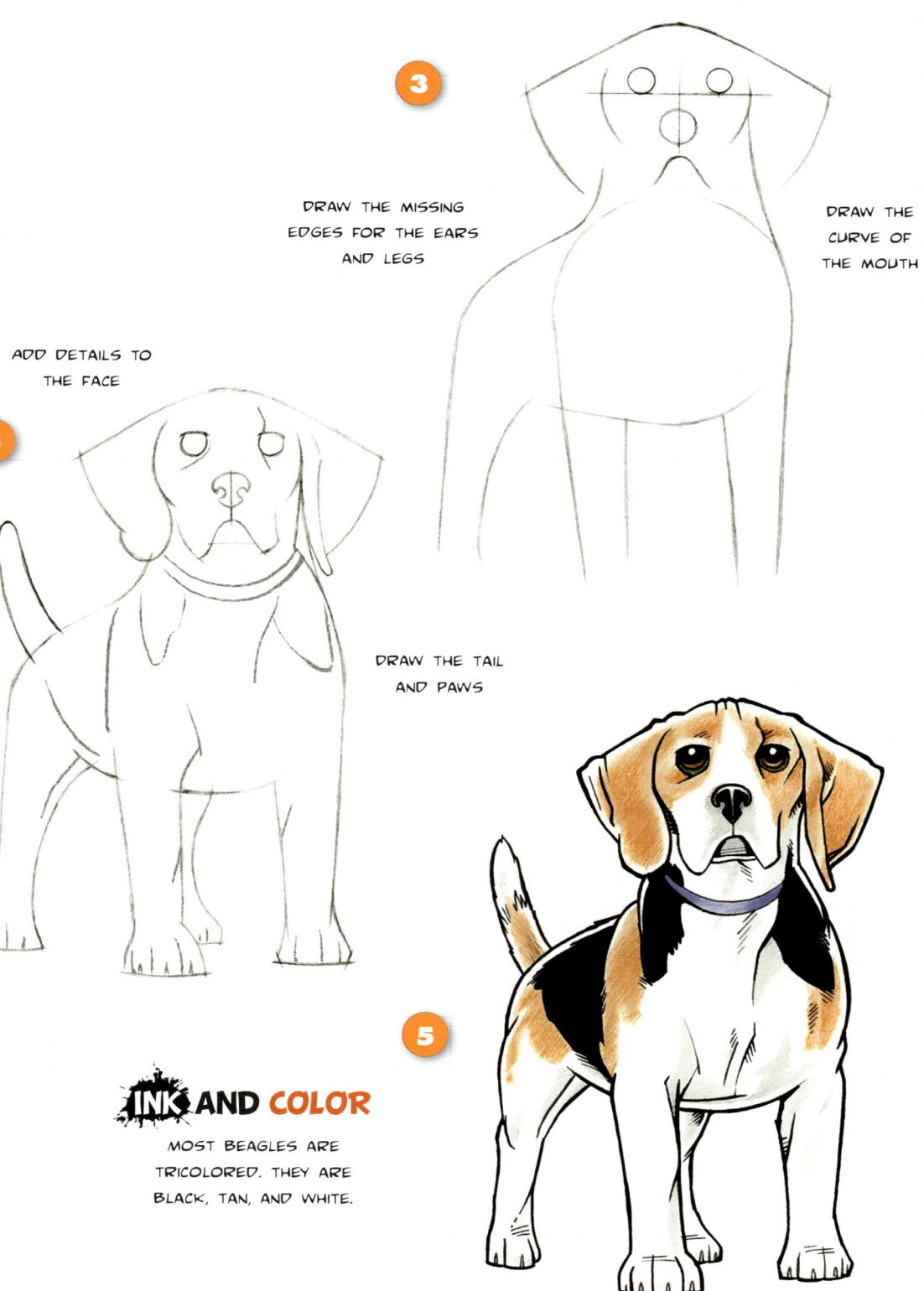

3 DRAW THE MISSING EDGES FOR THE EARS AND LEGS

DRAW THE CURVE OF THE MOUTH

4 ADD DETAILS TO THE FACE

DRAW THE TAIL AND PAWS

5 INK AND COLOR

MOST BEAGLES ARE TRICOLORED. THEY ARE BLACK, TAN, AND WHITE.

Labrador Retriever
The Bird Dog

The Labrador Retriever has been the most popular dog breed in the United States for over twenty years. Hunters value this active breed for its ability to retrieve ducks, geese, and other **game birds**. Families enjoy the friendly, gentle nature of the breed. No matter its coat color, the Labrador Retriever is a standout!

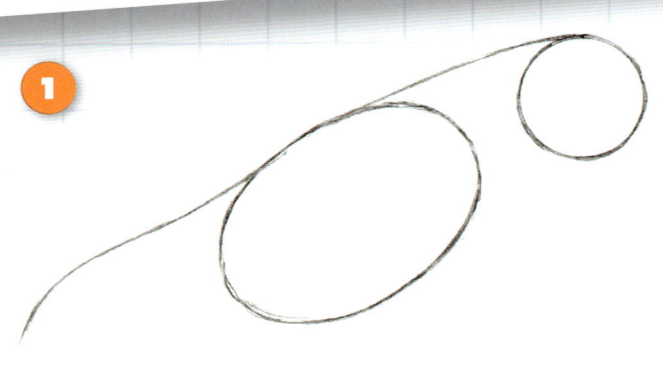

1

START WITH A SMALL CIRCLE FOR THE HEAD AND A LARGE OVAL FOR THE CHEST

SMUDGE IT

SMUDGING YOUR PENCIL MARKS WITH A WET FINGER OR SMUDGE STICK WILL GIVE YOU A VARIETY OF GRAY TONES.

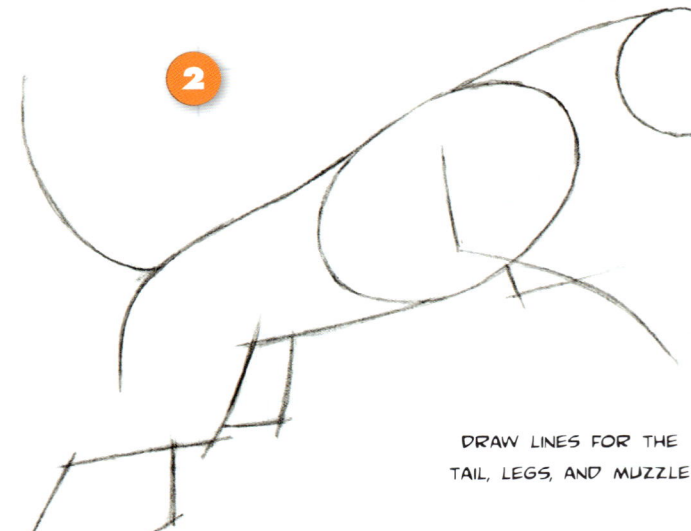

2

DRAW LINES FOR THE TAIL, LEGS, AND MUZZLE

Dalmatian
The Spotted Dog

Long associated with fire stations and firefighters, Dalmatians have a spotted coat pattern that anyone would recognize. Dalmatians often work as rescue dogs or service dogs. However, most people enjoy keeping them as loving family pets. Who wouldn't want to own a dog that can smile?

LIGHT TO DARK

Begin your drawing with very light lines. Slowly build up to dark lines as you reach the final steps. This will allow for easy correction of mistakes.

1 Begin with a small circle for the head and an oval for the chest. Draw a curved line for the back.

2 Lightly add lines for the legs, tail, and neck.

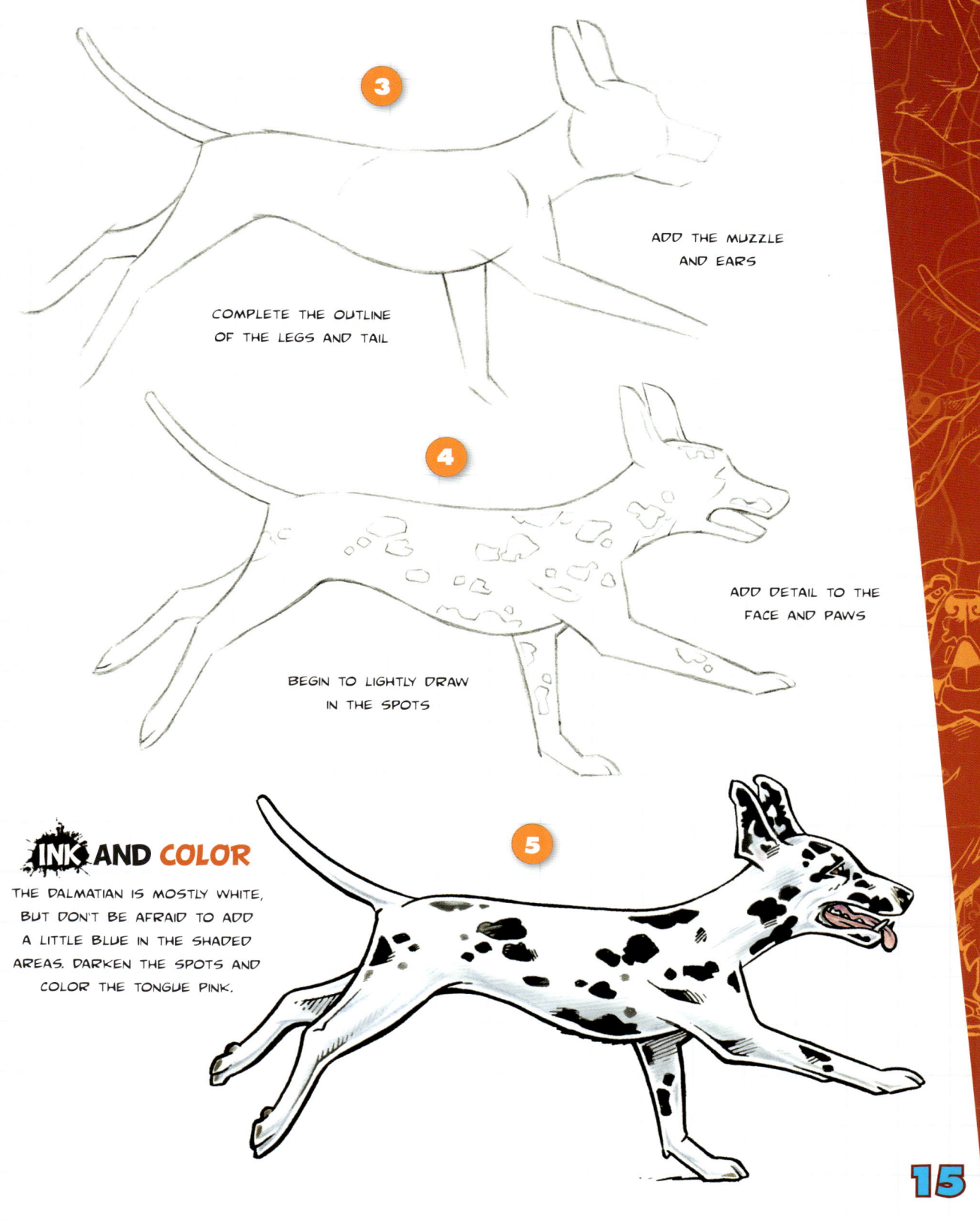

Doberman Pinscher
The Guard Dog

Dobermans are born with floppy ears. While they are still young, many have their ears **cropped**. This practice results in the sharply perked ears that give the breed a fierce and obedient look. Alert and fearless, Dobermans make excellent guard dogs. To strangers they are a threat, but to their owners they are loyal friends!

BEGIN WITH A LARGE CIRCLE FOR THE HEAD AND A SMALLER CIRCLE FOR THE MUZZLE

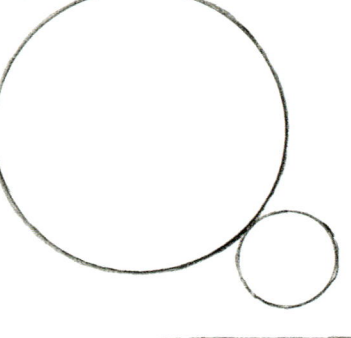

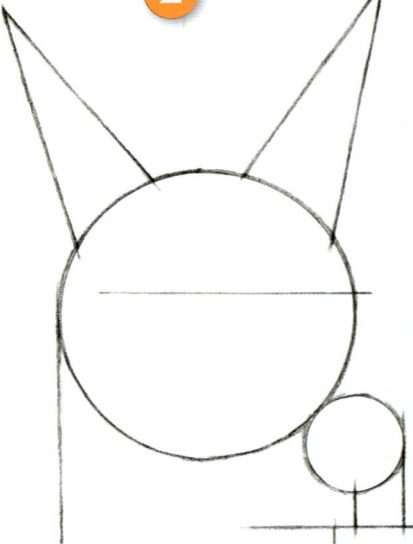

ADD THE NECK AND POINTED EARS

KEEP YOUR EDGE!

TO AVOID SHARPENING TOO MUCH, ROTATE YOUR PENCIL SLIGHTLY TO FIND A SHARP EDGE.

3

DRAW THE TOP EDGE OF THE MUZZLE AND THE CURVE OF THE MOUTH

4

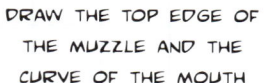

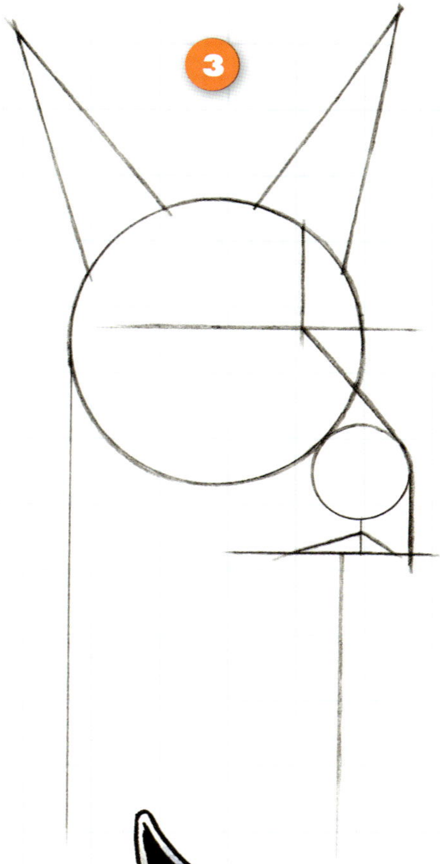

SHAPE THE OUTLINE OF THE EARS AND NOSE

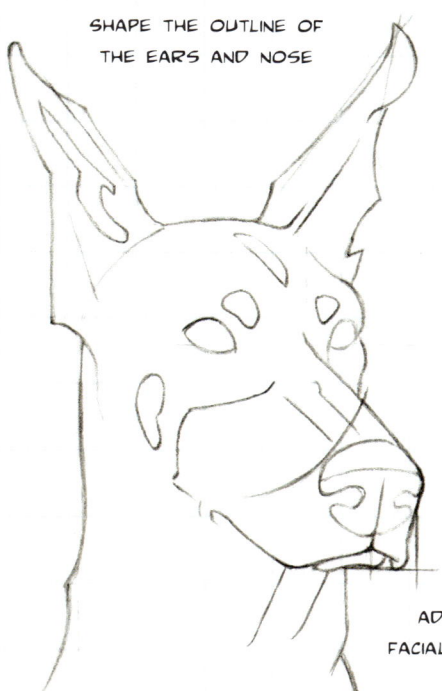

ADD THE FACIAL DETAILS

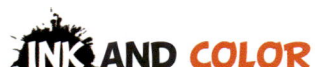

INK AND COLOR

DOBERMAN PINSCHERS ARE MOSTLY BLACK WITH SMALL AREAS OF TAN. ADD A LITTLE BLUE TO THE BLACK AREAS FOR A RICHER COLOR.

5

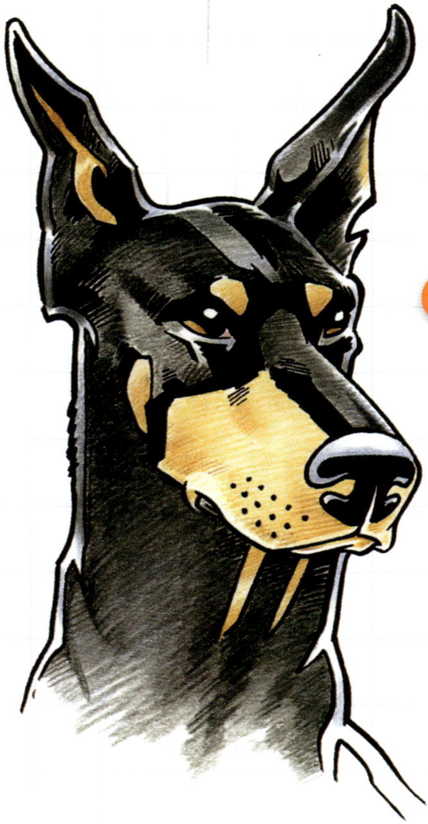

German Shepherd
The Service Dog

Strong and intelligent, German Shepherds love a challenge. This obedient breed craves exercise and the company of people. Their loyal and protective **temperament** makes them popular **guide dogs**. A keen sense of smell helps them excel in **search and rescue** and police work. German Shepherds are courageous companions to have by your side!

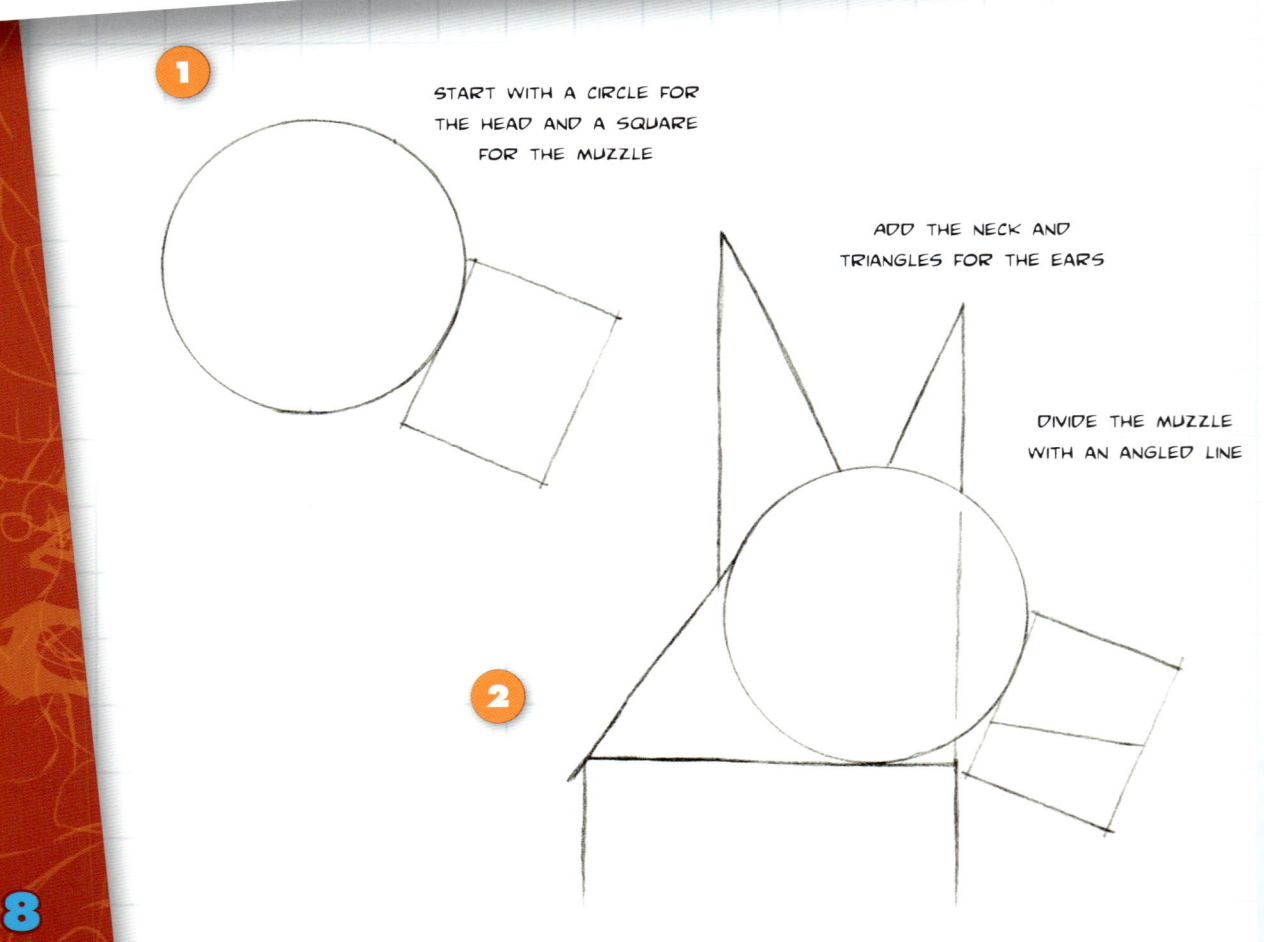

1. START WITH A CIRCLE FOR THE HEAD AND A SQUARE FOR THE MUZZLE

2. ADD THE NECK AND TRIANGLES FOR THE EARS

DIVIDE THE MUZZLE WITH AN ANGLED LINE

Chihuahua
The Toy Dog

Chihuahuas are small dogs with feisty personalities. This **toy breed** does well in **Teacup Agility** competitions. Their size and speed get them past obstacles in record time. At home, Chihuahuas are playful and loving toward their owners but suspicious of strangers. Don't get on the wrong side of a Chihuahua!

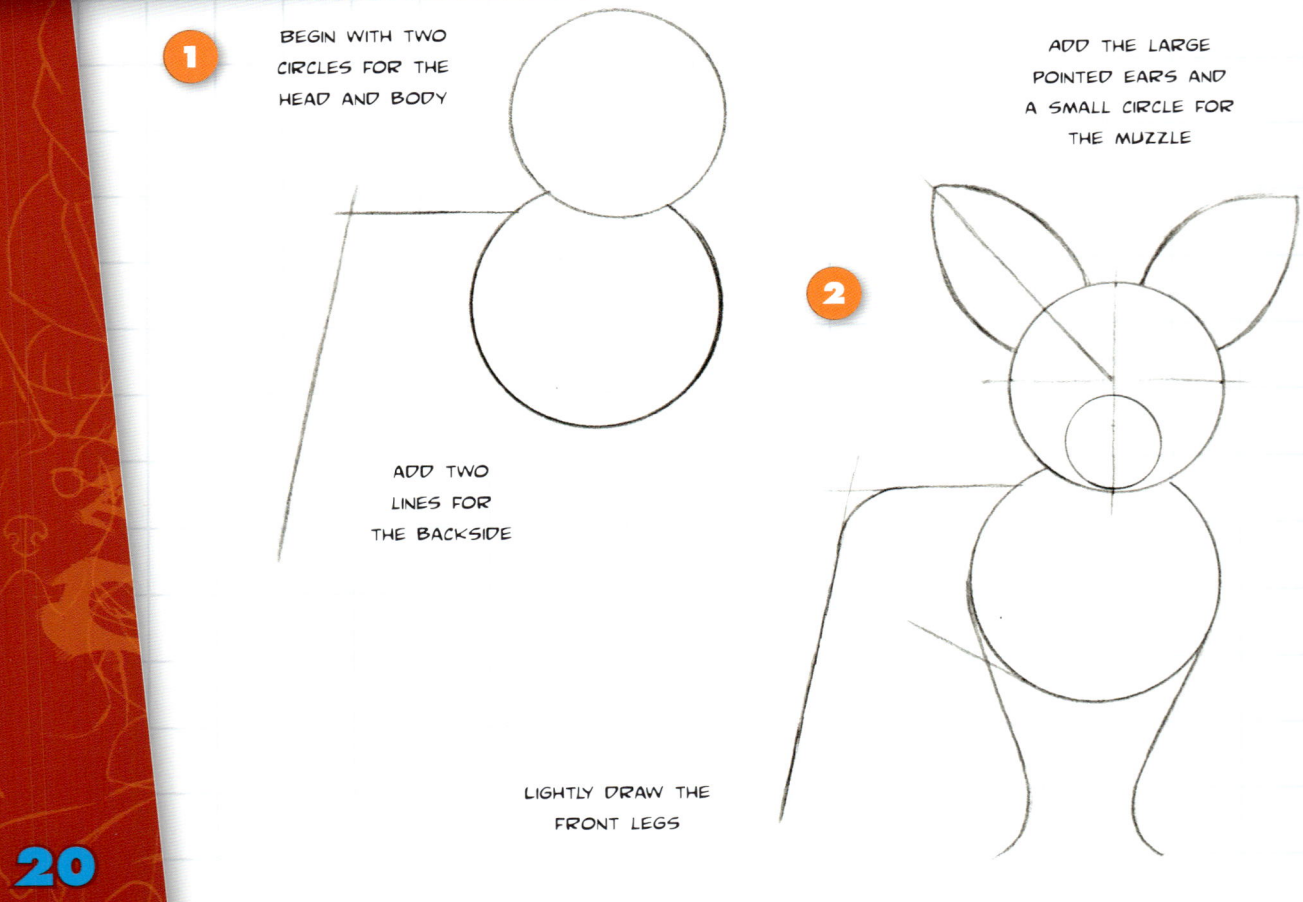

1. BEGIN WITH TWO CIRCLES FOR THE HEAD AND BODY

ADD TWO LINES FOR THE BACKSIDE

LIGHTLY DRAW THE FRONT LEGS

2. ADD THE LARGE POINTED EARS AND A SMALL CIRCLE FOR THE MUZZLE

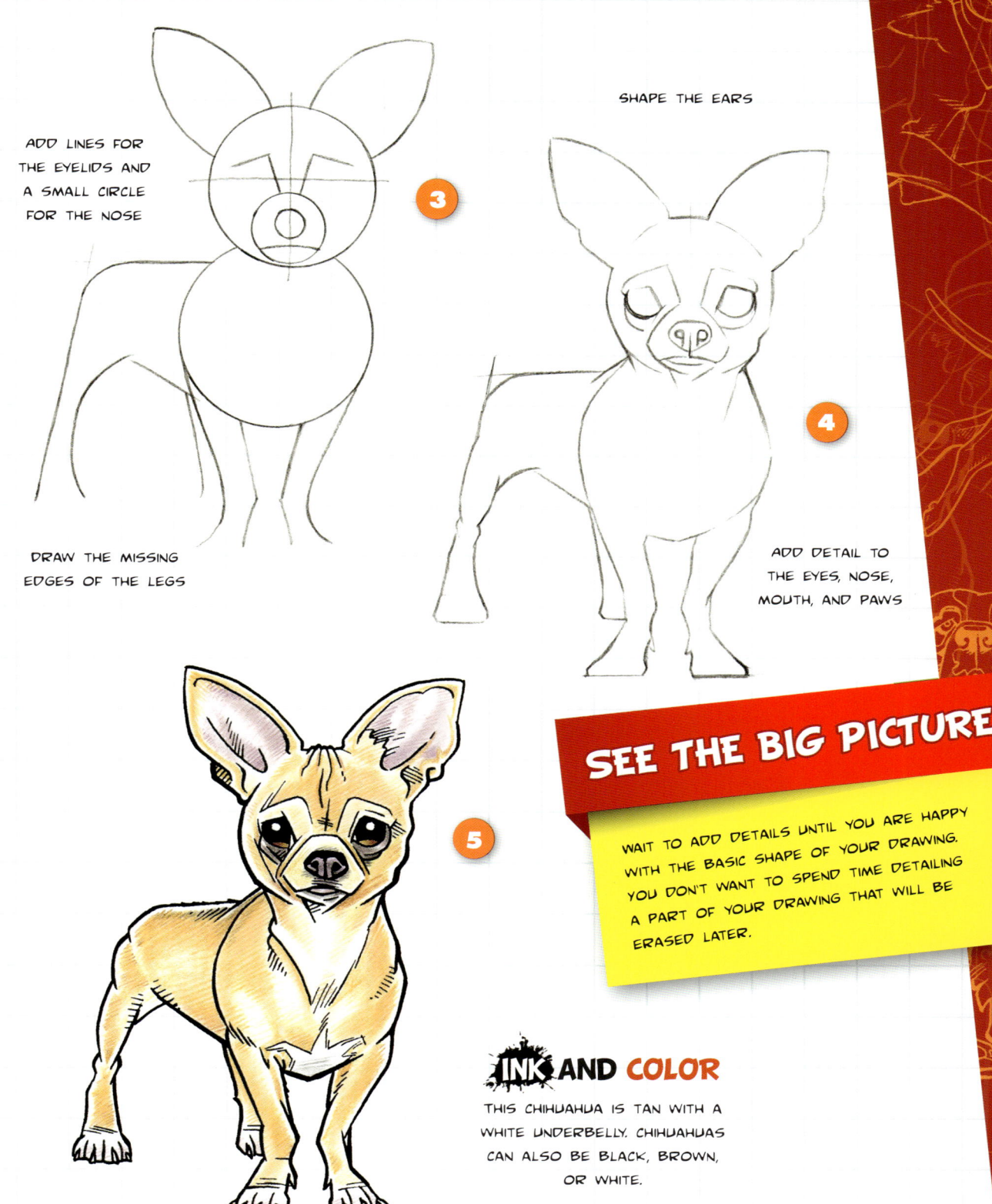

ADD LINES FOR THE EYELIDS AND A SMALL CIRCLE FOR THE NOSE

SHAPE THE EARS

3

DRAW THE MISSING EDGES OF THE LEGS

4

ADD DETAIL TO THE EYES, NOSE, MOUTH, AND PAWS

5

SEE THE BIG PICTURE

WAIT TO ADD DETAILS UNTIL YOU ARE HAPPY WITH THE BASIC SHAPE OF YOUR DRAWING. YOU DON'T WANT TO SPEND TIME DETAILING A PART OF YOUR DRAWING THAT WILL BE ERASED LATER.

INK AND COLOR

THIS CHIHUAHUA IS TAN WITH A WHITE UNDERBELLY. CHIHUAHUAS CAN ALSO BE BLACK, BROWN, OR WHITE.

GLOSSARY

agility—the ability to move quickly and easily

canine—relating to dogs

cropped—shaped by cutting

domesticated—trained to be comfortable around humans

game birds—birds that are hunted for sport

guide dogs—dogs trained to lead the blind

herd—to gather animals together and lead them

muzzles—the noses, mouths, and jaws of some animals

scent hounds—dogs that track prey by scent

search and rescue—the work of locating and saving missing people

Teacup Agility—an agility sport for small dog breeds

temperament—personality or nature

toy breed—a breed of dog that weighs less than 20 pounds (9 kilograms)

weight pulling—a dog sport in which dogs pull carts filled with weights

TO LEARN MORE

At the Library

Crosby, Jeff. *Little Lions, Bull Baiters & Hunting Hounds: A History of Dog Breeds.* Toronto, Ont.: Tundra Books, 2008.

Murawski, Laura. *How to Draw Dogs.* New York, N.Y.: PowerKids Press, 2001.

Stein, Garth. *Racing in the Rain.* New York, N.Y.: Harper, 2011.

On the Web

Learning more about dogs is as easy as 1, 2, 3.

1. Go to www.factsurfer.com.

2. Enter "dogs" into the search box.

3. Click the "Surf" button and you will see a list of related Web sites.

With factsurfer.com, finding more information is just a click away.

INDEX

adding details, 21
Beagle, 10-11
Chihuahua, 20-21
Dalmatian, 14-15
Doberman Pinscher, 16-17
drawing from photos, 4
drawing lightly, 5, 14
German Shepherd, 18-19
holding the pencil, 16
Labrador Retriever, 12-13
left-handed, 9
mixing colors, 19
Pug, 6-7
right-handed, 9
Saint Bernard, 8-9
smudging, 5, 9, 12
supplies, 5
using basic shapes, 6
using your arm, 10